My First
Spanish
Lesson

Color & Learn!

Illustrated by
Roz Fulcher

Te quiero.
teh kee-**eh**-roh

Dover Publications, Inc.
Mineola, New York

This handy book will have you speaking Spanish in no time! More than sixty illustrated pages include commonly used words and phrases in both Spanish and English. Below each Spanish word or phrase you'll find its pronunciation. A syllable that is **boldfaced** should be stressed.

Whether it's just for fun, for travel, or to have a conversation with a friend or relative, you'll find out how to talk about the weather, tell what you'd like at mealtime, and many other helpful phrases—and you can color while you learn!

Bibliographical Note

This Dover edition, first published in 2019, is a republication in a different format of the work originally published by Dover in 2015 as *Color & Learn Easy Spanish Phrases for Kids*.

International Standard Book Number

ISBN-13: 978-0-486-83309-5
ISBN-10: 0-486-83309-7

Manufactured in the United States by LSC Communications
83309701   2019
www.doverpublications.com

Hello.   *Good-bye.*

See you later.

Es mi   *1. madre*   *2. padre*
ess mee   **mah**-dreh   **pah**-dreh

3. hermana   *4. hermano*
ehr-**mah**-nah   ehr-**mah**-noh

This is my   1. Mother   2. Father

3. Sister   4. Brother

I'm allergic to nuts/eggs.

I love you.

What's for breakfast?   1. Cereal

2. pan tostado
pahn tohs-**tah**-doh

3. huevos
weh-bohs

2. Toast   3. Eggs

1. un sándwich
oon **sahnd**-weech

It's time for lunch. I want. . .

1. a sandwich

2. un yogur
oon yoh-**goor**

3. una hamburguesa
oo-nah ahm-boor-**geh**-sah

2. Yogurt   3. Hamburger

13

I'm hungry! What's for dinner?

1. ¿Pollo?
poh-yoh

2. ¿Pescado?
pehs-**kah**-doh

3. ¿Pizza?
peet-sah

1. Chicken?   2. Fish?   3. Pizza?

What's for dessert?

1. helado
eh-**lah**-doh

2. fruta
froo-tah

3. galletas
gah-**yeh**-tahs

1. Ice cream   2. Fruit
3. Cookies

4. pasear en bicicleta
pah-seh-**ahr** ehn bee-see-**kleh**-tah

3. dibujar
dee-boo-**hahr**

3. Draw   4. Bike

Can you help me, please? I'm lost.

¡Feliz Navidad!

feh-**lees** nah-bee-**dahd**

Merry Christmas!

¡Feliz Año Nuevo!

feh-lees ah-nyoh **nweh**-boh!

Happy New Year!

This is delicious! I'd like some more.

Los días de la semana.

los **dee**-ahs deh lah seh-**mah**-nah

Monday

lunes
loo-nehs

Tuesday

martes
mahr-tehs

Wednesday

miercoles
mee-**ehr**-koh-lehs

Days of the week

Thursday   *jueves*
hweh-behs

Friday   *viernes*
bee-**ehr**-nehs

Saturday   *sábado*
sah-bah-doh

Sunday   *domingo*
doh-**meen**-goh

Los meses
lohs **meh**-sehs

January

enero
eh-**neh**-roh

February

febrero
feh-**breh**-roh

March

marzo
mahr-soh

April

abril
ah-**breel**

May

mayo
mah-yoh

June

junio
hoo-nee-oh

Months

julio
hoo-lee-yoh

agosto
ah-**gohs**-toh

septiembre
sehp-tee-**ehm**-breh

octubre
ohk-**too**-breh

noviembre
noh-bee-**ehm**-breh

diciembre
dee-see-**ehm**-breh

Los números
lohs **noo**-meh-rohss

uno
oo-noh

dos
dohs

tres
trehs

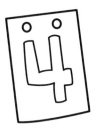 

cuatro
kwah-troh

cinco
seen-koh

Numbers

seis
sehs

siete
see-**eh**-teh

ocho
oh-choh

nueve
noo-**eh**-beh

diez
dee-**ehs**

Los colores
lohs koh-**loh**-rehs

Green
verde
behr-deh

Red
rojo
roh-hoh

Blue
azul
ah-**sool**

Yellow
amarillo
ah-mah-**ree**-yoh

Colors

Colors

32

White
blanco
blahn-koh

Black
negro
neh-groh

Orange
anaranjado
ah-nah-rahn-**hah**-doh

Purple
morado
moh-**rah**-doh

Gray
gris
greess

1. How much does it cost?

2. It's one dollar.

Let's go to the beach! I will get . . .

1. traje de baño
trah-heh deh **bah**-nyoh

2. loción
loh-see-**ohn**

3. toalla
toh-**ah**-yah

1. my bathing suit   2. my lotion
3. my towel

Please.

Thank you.   You're welcome.

Could you speak more slowly?

It's hot today. I'll wear . . .

1. una camiseta
oo-nah kah-mee-**seh**-tah

2. unos pantalones cortos
oo-nohs pahn-tah-**loh**-nehs
kohr-tohs

3. unas sandalias
oo-nahs sahn-**dah**-lee-ahs

1. a T-shirt   2. shorts
3. sandals

43

It's snowing! I need . . .

1. mi bufanda
mee boo-**fahn**-dah

2. mis guantes
mees **gwahn**-tehs

3. mis botas
mees **boh**-tahs

4. mi abrigo
mee ah-**bree**-goh

1. my scarf

2. my gloves

3. my boots

4. my coat

1. un suéter
oon **sweh**-tehr

2. una manta
oo-nah **mahn**-tah

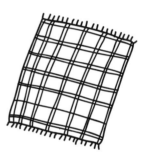

3. una chaqueta
oo-nah chah-**keh**-tah

1. a sweater　　2. a blanket
3. a jacket

Do you speak English?

Sorry, I don't understand.

1. agua
ah-gwah

2. jugo
hoo-goh

3. leche
leh-cheh

1. water   2. juice   3. milk

Excuse me. Where is the nearest . . .

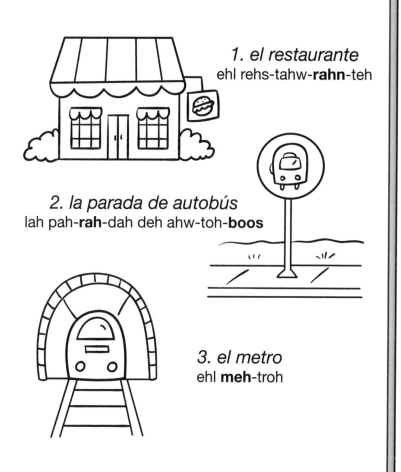

1. el restaurante
ehl rehs-tahw-**rahn**-teh

2. la parada de autobús
lah pah-**rah**-dah deh ahw-toh-**boos**

3. el metro
ehl **meh**-troh

1. restaurant?   2. bus stop?

3. subway?

Do you have a pet?   I have a . . .

1. perro
peh-roh

2. gato
gah-toh

3. pez
pays

4. pájaro
pah-hah-roh

5. hámster
ahm-stehr

1. dog   2. cat   3. fish
4. bird   5. hamster

Happy birthday! My birthday is in

_____.

1. ver la televisión
behr lah
teh-leh-bee-see-**ohn**

2. ir al cine
eer ahl **see**-neh

3. salir afuera
sah-**leer** ah-**fweh**-rah

¿Puedo . . .?
pweh-doh

Can I . . . 1. Watch TV?
2. Go to a movie? 3. Go outside?

1. abuela
ah-**bway**-lah

2. abuelo
ah-**bway**-loh

3. tía
tee-ah

4. tío
tee-oh

5. prima
pree-mah

6. primo
pree-moh

1. Grandma

2. Grandpa

3. Aunt

4. Uncle

5. Cousin (girl)

6. Cousin (boy)

I don't feel well. My . . . 1. throat
2. head   3. stomach . . . (hurts)

I'm tired. Time for bed.

Good night.